As the Crows So I

As the Crows So I

Poems by Liz Gorrie

SilverWood

Published in paperback by SilverWood Books 2012
www.silverwoodbooks.co.uk

Text copyright © The Estate of Liz Gorrie 2012

For the purposes of authenticity the poems in this book have been published exactly
as the author intended, with no correction other than a light proofread.

ISBN 978-1-78132-018-1

British Library Cataloguing in Publication Data
A CIP catalogue record for this book is available from the British Library

Set in Goudy Old Style by SilverWood Books
Printed on paper sourced responsibly

Front cover: This illustration was used in a promotional brochure for *Kaleidophonics* –
a children's introduction to the Orchestra. Performed in front of a full orchestra, this was one of
Liz's favourite creations, of which she presented eight versions over her years with her theatre
company. The music performed for each of the images shown in this illustration was:
Susato's Brass Quintet – the yellow jester starts to play and gently pulls the strings;
Ponchielli's Dance of the Hours – the mushrooms dance while Pan gives chase;
Stravinsky's Firebird Suite – the fire witch screams her primal cry, the serpent coils its tail;
Gershwin's Summertime – soft summer winds ripple the pond,
a young boy with fishing rod dreams.

Contents

Introduction

Liz started to write early in her theatre career. She wanted to explore new ways to reach her audiences, new ways in which to tell stories on stage. As her producer for most of her plays, I was very much involved with her work, but less so with her poetry. She would sometimes read me a poem for my comments, but if I asked for more, they weren't ready or they needed more work.

I became more involved in what I had felt was her personal writing after she left the theatre in 2000. She had lost a book of her writings, which we never found, and I wasn't going to let that happen again. So I started to file her poems on my computer. She was a pen and ink writer. From scrapes of paper and loose sheets started to accumulate a body of work.

Liz touched many lives through her work in theatre. She was admired and loved for the encouragement that she gave, the challenges that she offered and her 'joie de vivre'.

Friends and relatives knew her as an outgoing, fun seeking extrovert with a strong sense of humour. Few knew this other side of her personality, a side that challenged accepted dogma, grieved many aspects of the human condition, and did not ignore the ugly side of life. Liz never passed a street person without giving a smile, a kind word and whatever change she had in her pocket (*The Dumpster Queen* and *Old Brown Grey Man*).

Her poetry expressed this 'private' side of her life, exploring some of those questions for which we all search answers, but seldom express what we find as well as she did. (*Easter Requiem 1 & 2*) She was, of course, a feminist, but drew her convictions more from her knowledge of history (*Morgana*) than her own career. She questioned where the movement might lead (*New Liberated Woman*). She expressed emotions about which she felt deeply, but which she kept to herself, (*Gypsy Go Home*) and as a fourth generation Canadian she had a deep understanding and love of myth and cultural roots (*Wiltshire*).

For me this book of poems is a further recognition of the talented, complex and creative woman that I loved and I would like to share that recognition with those who knew and loved her too, those who admired her work in theatre and those who appreciate a mind that questioned and challenged through poetry.

Colin Gorrie
January 2012, Bristol

This promotional head shot was taken when Liz was contracted to work in film in Vancouver after she retired from the theatre.

Liz Gorrie 1941–2011

She was a wartime baby, born in Kitchener, Ontario, on August 29, 1941, and baptised Elizabeth Diana Douglas Wallace. Her father, Hal, was a high school teacher. He had represented Canada at the 1932 Los Angeles Olympics in the country's Lacrosse team. Her mother, Ethelynn (known as Lynn), was also an athlete in a generation when women were taking on new societal roles. Her 100 yard dash record stayed unchallenged on her high school notice board for well over 20 years. Lynn had the intelligence and energy to take up a profession, but remained a mother and housewife for her family, and lived her life vicariously through her daughter. Their relationship would be strained for much of their lives.

Elizabeth, or Liz as she preferred, was one of those lucky people who knew what they wanted to do in life from a very early age. She recounted with laughter how she would organise the neighbourhood kids in 'productions' in the backyard. She had an unusual singing voice with a three octave range. Her older brother, Duncan, took piano lessons. Liz was given singing lessons. Her parents wanted her to be an opera singer, and in her early teens took her to see a Metropolitan Opera Company's touring production of *Aida*, but when Liz saw the title role played by a 250-pound diva the romance of that career option disintegrated. She set her sights on theatre, and was soon taking lead roles in her high school's musicals. She entered the University of Manitoba and was invited to be her College's "Freshie Queen", which she accepted somewhat reluctantly. Parading her beauty was not her style. She joined the University Glee Club, the only musical theatre option in Winnipeg at the time, and failed her first year, which was par for the course in those days. However, studying was easy for her when she was so inclined, and within a year she was passing her courses, taking lead roles, and had started a budding romance with her leading man. She graduated with an honours degree in English and History in 1963, married her leading man, and took a social service job, so her husband could complete his degree. But the experience that started what was to become a future career was her summer job while at University, Playground Drama Supervisor for the Winnipeg Parks Board.

Two children followed. Gavin born in 1966 (*Gavin 1975*) and Katya born 18 months later. (*Katya 1975*) Returning from a year in the UK where her husband was on scholarship, Liz was determined that her first theatre would explore new territory. Within a couple of months she had taken over Total Theatre Brantford, a new community theatre group seeking professional leadership. What is extraordinary is that a small, conservative town in rural Ontario would accept, indeed embrace, an experimental theatre group. It very much speaks to the personality of its leader. Liz presented playwrights like Jean-Claude van Itallie, the seminal force of the explosive Off-Broadway Theatre of the sixties, not with the anger and commitment of most young experimental theatre directors of the late sixties, but with the smile and sense of humour that invited participation. The palate for her theatre included all the disciplines – mime, mask, movement, dance, puppetry and voice.

Following her husband's new job on the West Coast, her next move was to form Bastion's Studio Theatre Company in Victoria on Vancouver Island. An experimental arm for a regional theatre company was a first for Canada. Adapting a second floor commercial storage area as a performance space in the centre of town, Liz was soon at work again. Ibsen's *Peer Gynt*, Marowwitz's *Hamlet*, Euripides' *Trojan Women*, and Lee and Lawrence's *The Night Thoreau Spent in Jail*, were not the usual entertainment fare in British Columbia's sleepy capital city. Not that Liz had forgotten her love of musical theatre, which saw her as the lead in a couple of summer musical productions. But the focus of her work as a director was to mould her actors into an ensemble based on Grotowski's work in Europe. However, this type of exploration is too often short-lived, and when the government funding ran out, it was back to Winnipeg, where work was available.

Moving back to prairie winters from the beauty and mild climate of Canada's west coast was not easy, (*Winnipeg in January*) but Liz made an opportunity of it. She landed a job as a television interviewer and the first female summer replacement TV weather announcer for the Canadian Broadcasting Corporation. For her weather broadcasts she developed her own signature on camera. Wet your finger, hold it up and then tell your audience the wind velocity and direction. It wasn't long before people started greeting her with this signature on the bus. But this was 1973 and she had landed herself into the centre of an exclusively male profession. Liz was a feminist, not strident, unless provoked. She had not carved out a female theatre directorship for herself, one of the first in Canada, for any political reason. She merely believed that ability and qualification should dictate career, not gender, and she felt it was high time for society to acknowledge this reality. (*New Liberated Woman*) The stay in Winnipeg was mercifully cut short. An invitation arrived for her to take the artistic leadership of a new Theatre for Young Audiences back on the West Coast. Her career was set.

Kaleidoscope Theatre gained swift national recognition. Liz's adaptation of Paul Galico's short story, *The Snow Goose*, was an immediate, national success. The lead role, the Goose, was an abstract trio of large bird-like wings of stretched cotton on metal frames manipulated on rods by three actors. *The Snow Goose* was received with standing ovations at an international ASSITEJ conference in Montreal. Even in the 70s this genre of theatre had no body of literature to draw on, and very few playwrights serving its market, particularly in Canada. What little was being produced was either too verbose or condescending for Liz's taste. Speaking at some event she once said; "We look at the clouds in the morning and wonder if we should take our umbrellas. Children see those clouds as chariots, dragons and monsters. It is that creative imagination that we are born with that my theatre can help to nourish." When the Canada Council dubbed her work as 'Theatre of Imagery' the title stuck. Today this style of theatre is widely used. Exploring the style half a century ago Liz was a pioneer in the field. In 1977 she was awarded the Queen's Silver Jubilee Medal for her contribution to Canadian Theatre for Young Audiences.

Liz's theatre rehearsing technique was unusual and often bordered on chaotic. She expected her actors to find their own way to their character development, which was not the style for most theatre directors of the day. If she didn't agree with the results, she had that knack of convincing actors that her interpretation was really theirs. A quote from a recent email of condolences summed it up differently. "…To me her ability to create belief and enthusiasm was more than I have seen in anyone." As an actor, "I was one of many who wanted to help clear a path for her imagination and vision…and, incidentally, to hear the most beautiful laugh from a most beautiful person." It was Liz's idea to initiate an International Performing Arts Festival for Young Audiences, and when Victoria City Hall turned down the idea, Vancouver picked it up. It was this Festival that spawned many similar festivals across Canada, the Northern States and Scotland.

For over 20 years Liz created, adapted and directed over 50 theatre pieces with Kaleidoscope. For her youngest audiences she explored the techniques of animating inanimate objects. Her scripts focused on dramatic action rather than dialogue. She wanted to feed their creative imaginations. Titles like *Salt the Seas and Pepper your Mints*, *Where Umbrellas Bloom*, or *The Allihipporhinocrocadiligator* paint that picture. She loved myth and epic and was a great fan of Joseph Campbell's work, and for those critical, intermediate ages she excited them with titles like *The Legend of the Minotaur*, *Merlin's Quest*, and adaptations of two of Ursula Le Guin's *Earthsea* novels. For teenagers she presented a theatre that was relevant to them. Her *Romeo and Juliet* was set on the West Bank with the love affair between a Jewish boy and Palestinian girl, and where appropriate long speeches of descriptive dialogue were replaced with dramatic imagery. She created *Stilletto*, a daring piece that some teachers boycotted, dealing with cruelty, violence and sex that had become part of the teenage world, and she explored the science of Astrophysics in a play entitled *Diner at the end of the Galaxy*.

In 1991 she finally got her own 300 seat theatre, after years of creating productions for touring. Her work had travelled extensively through Canada and the States, but with a facility she could use her palette of disciplines to the full. Kaleidoscope was the first Canadian theatre company to tour Japan, and two of her plays were picked up by the National Theatre for Young Audiences in Tel Aviv. She was invited to Israel to direct them in Hebrew, of which she didn't speak a word, but loved its rich and musical sound. "It makes my dialogue sound much more beautiful than it really is."

Liz loved cooking, which became an excuse for elaborate dinner parties, elaborate because if the conversations were not interesting, guests found themselves playing games at the dinner table. "Botticelli" and "Murder", played at the same time, was a favourite. She loved wine, so making one's own wine became a family necessity. She dressed elegantly, but her wardrobe was usually second hand, and second hand clothes shops were her idea a shopping spree. She loved to travel, but the journeys were always somewhat unplanned, allowing circumstances to dictate along the way.

When she lost her theatre in 2000 because the City would not buy the building from a new owner who wanted to change it into a commercial property, it was time to leave Victoria, and, as it turned out, leave her profession. But she continued to write poetry. It was her way of expressing those emotions that she rarely expressed verbally – her anger, her sadness, and her frustrations. But her poetry also captures her joy, her love, and her everlasting sense of humour, and it will be her poetry for which she will be remembered particularly for those who did not know her work in theatre.

Liz died on August 3, 2011, in Bristol, (*As the Crows So I*) after battling cancer for two years. Some of her ashes were scattered by her English family and friends from the top of Glastonbury Tor. Her Canadian family and friends scattered some of her ashes in West hawk Lake, her family's summer cottage playground in Manitoba, and a third scattering was made by her theatre friends and partners into the Pacific Ocean off Victoria, British Columbia.

Beginnings

Beginnings

Liz was born a blond, but her theatre career gave her an excuse to change when she felt like it, long before it became fashionable.

The Tree

Autumn dusk
small child's cloth
hangs from tightly held
fingers of the tree
a trophy
dancing with the moving branch

He's a wise old friend
that tree
guarding children's games
loving as they nestle against his trunk
for rest
murmuring stories of other children
long ago
do they day dream
sitting there under his branches?

Each autumn
this green-yellow-checkered trophy
hangs on bare branches
the winter is long
his children come no more
he is lonely.

A Valentine

Love
how to express
mine for you...
like wine
aged
becoming richer and deeper
Or
an amati violin
rare, and with age resounding
truer
Or
the seasons...
the spring passions
the summer richness
the autumn fulfillment
the winter...
No
these metaphors
tho' true
won't do

You are the air
breathe in
breathe out
my waking and
my sleeping
you have coloured my world
a thousand easels
couldn't capture
the rich tones of joy
and shades of despair
But...

if you walked through
the thousand easel surround
the gallery is filled
with the rich colours of love
dark shades
overshadowed
lost in the background
the reds and purples
bright yellows
stunning blues
sing such a song
the angels joined in too

The sound is so resounding
you feel the city quake
the earth quivers and trembles
in that enormous shake
Okay... okay... okay...
It's not so big
but somehow
I heard the angels sing
they loved the colours
we painted
through
summer, autumn, spring

The angels
are hovering
wings shimmering
in last light
waiting to know
what we'll do
with winter's night

In the Midst of Labour

Suddenly
in the midst of labour
a strain of music
catches the ear
gradually lifting
expanding the heart
to such a height
of ecstasy

Then
just as the climax
is about to explode
diminuendo sets in
slowly... easing
the pain/pleasure
leaving
a bittersweet melancholy
and tears
lying on the cheek

Christmas in Liverpool, 1967

A child born in the darkness of the year
shedding light and calm surrounding your being
an omen to your life's struggle –
you to keep the light in the midst of darkness
Me
too much light, searching the dark side
we've met deeply, often unspoken
on the edges
      of the chasm
our connection
      is deeper
           than art
        deeper than blood
           that holds the world

Tho' born in the darkness of the year
your being surrounds all with light
not like the morning star, which fades in the dawn
but the evening star
which glimmers brightly in the night sky
sparkling the mind with dreams of the possible
where the imagination takes flight.

Ed.
Liz's second child, Katya, was born in Liverpool in 1967.
She was reading Tolstoy's War and Peace *at the time.*

Gavin, 1974

Moving in the dream
light phosphorous places
of invisible gold swords
flying on winds of
          honourable gods
chasing patterns of
          reflected adventures
spreading wings of gentleness
winding down roads of innocence
through towns unblighted
by our lost vision
eyes bright with belief
          in the possible
always of the moment

What can we teach you
but to walk silent musty museums
waiting to learn
we teach you
          "thou shalt not!"

Your explorations by comparison
make Columbus an old man
with dark glasses and a cane
Hold on to your vision
my son
for only the
very wise old man
          understands.

Ed.
*Liz's son was born in Winnipeg in 1966. She chose Gavin, the Angli-
cized version of Gawain. He was 8 years old when she wrote this poem*

Katya, 1975

My little ancient princess
you carry in your heart
the terror of the merciless weird
and the tenderness
of boundless love

Moving through your secret world
becoming all ages
in a single moment
turning first your dark countenance
then your light

Dancing and whirling
through each moment
of now
the sunbeams dance with you
all into my heart

Winnipeg in January

Cold, ugly city
building steel and glass ramparts of death
to hold out the vast prairie
were you so afraid for your existence
in this blue/white void?

You have shocked lady nature
by your dismissal
and now unaware of slow starvation
in solitary confinement
it's in your eyes – in your feet
as you plod, heads bowed
down wide, windy spaces
hearts so frail
they are whisked away by the smallest gust
pretending protection from huge, grey slabs

Why didn't you guess
when there was only reflections of shadows from glass?
why didn't you guess
even the white bright snowsun
ignores you
having nothing to play on
why didn't you guess
his magic is not strong enough
against your death.

So he looks on
with a half-hearted stare
dreaming of other places where he can dance.

Cold city
there is no place to dream
I can only remember that I forgot.

Ed.
Liz's family lived in Winnipeg from 1953 – 1965, where she
attended High School and University. She expressed her response
to the City, when she returned for 2 years in 1973.

Our Journey

Please come with me
nowhere and everywhere
I know now I must go
but I need your light
to transform the path

For we are one
you and I
and when separated
the split nerve ends
of our souls
shrivels a little
dangling in space
directionless...

I know it is so
for when your hand touches mine
the stars grow brighter
the branches gently nod their approval
the earth warms my feet
with love...

I need the closeness of your breath
to hear the rhythm of the earth
your body
to outline the space beyond

I am patient
and will wait
for our journey
        began long, long ago

Looking At Whys

Looking At Whys

These costume sketches designed by Mary Kerr were for a Kaleidoscope production of *The Tempest*. Mary and Liz collaborated for this unusual production of Shakespeare's play that was performed at the Theatre Department of the University of Victoria during the 1984–85 season.

A Lazy Thought

There go the grown ups
to the office
to the store
subway rush
traffic crush
hurry, scurry
worry, flurry

There go the grown ups
heads kept down
heart rate up
button pushers
queuing jams
pressure cooking
body slams

No wonder
grown ups
don't grow up
anymore

It takes a lot
of slow
to grow.

Wiltshire 2005

Old stones
old bones
old truths
leveled by the wind

She's walked these hills
a blue mantled gown
shifting and lifting the earth
the old stones knew her
bowed down as she passed
then the dark horsemen came
and day passed into night

She fed a solstice fire
oak leaves in her hair
the fire started to burn
but just as the light
brightened the night
the dark horsemen came
and day passed into night

She lay in agony
a young queen trying to cope
screaming for the progeny
the king and country's hope
the stones remained silent
as day passed into night

She was led to the pyre
with jeers, fears of delight
a young country girl
who could feel
who could heal
still the dark horsemen came
as day passed into night

She walked into hallowed halls
the doors slammed tightly shut
the dark horsemen
have left their steeds
now history, tradition is enough
words and laws can keep her at bay
as night turns into
a murky day

Then she raises her head
in a most unseemly manner
chains and starves herself
instead of being the hostess
with glamour
the old horsemen
sputter, embarrassed and fuming
a few take a whip
others brandy and gloomy

continued...

She lies, vein-tubed
in a hospital bed
alone and dying
her family dispersed
but a smile
so weak
defines her face
the stones have shifted
she sees the end of the curse
as night passes into day

On a cold winter night
a young woman walks out
something is strange
a warm wind about
swirling and shifting
a weight has been lifted
she stares at the sky
she doesn't know why
and her feet start to
dance
as night passes into day

Old stones
old bones
old truths
leveled by the wind

No one has noticed
the stones have shifted
one has split wide open
no one hears
the old bones laughing
'cause the wind has covered that too

And the dark horsemen
well, they've died in their gin
or caught in their company scams
yes they're still there in spades
running democracy parades
or still guerilla boys
blowing up their kin
but night has passed into day

Notes on Wiltshire 2005
written by the author

Verse 1
The ancient earth mother, often in old myths is blue clad,
nourisher, embodiment of female mysteries

Verse 2
The same goddess in Celtic guise, fertility goddess of
man(woman), animals, crops. She was the first among deities

Verse 3
Based primarily on European royal houses (but I'm sure it's
universal) – kings married women to provide sons – then discarded
if they didn't do their job

Verse 4
*Refers to women trying to enter 'men's only' institutions –
universities, business, science, even the arts*

Verse 5
*Refers to women who spearheaded the suffragette movement –
many coming from aristocratic or upper middle class backgrounds*

Verse 6
*A contemporary woman, dying of old age – her family dispersed –
lonely but knowing a battle has been won – a balance is coming into
being*

The last verses
*A young woman, not necessarily aware of the enormous battle
of the centuries to bring the earth and it's inhabitants back into
balance, is standing on such a rich history of the goddesses?
Domain yet feels a power stirring
And the horsemen? We know who they are!*

Ed.
*Although this poem was written years later, Liz had claimed her
Celtic heritage as a young woman and had delved into the deep
roots of the feminist struggle.*

Dreams I

Moving through lonely, solitary places
weaving delicate, transparent threads
of dreams
which sparkle in the sun
swift momentary lights
flicker – then disappear
dreams –
like raindrops on branches
growing and bulging
until they explode and fall
finished… nothing
but for one glorious moment
full, sparkling, unique

Fog sets in
transforming the silver labyrinth
of threads
into heavy, lank nets
of green slime
caught…
struggling only tightens the trap
one can only wait
learning acceptance
of that awful limitation

continued…

There are no longer
marvelous swords or
mythical animals
to guide
the magic has been lost
buried deep in the ground
the dragon guarding
the treasure
fell asleep long ago
          through boredom
becoming flabby and wanton
with no combat.

So we wait
with vanishing dreams
dazzling the eye for a
moment
then lost
forever to wait.

Ed.
There are a number of poems, two more of which follow, that use
a theme of dreams. It seems to express the searching quest of the
creative mind under pressure to produce.

Dreams II

If I could only awaken
rummaging frantically through memories
with sleep drugged eyes
as if looking among countless files
of record jackets

I know its there
but I don't know what I'm looking for
I might have passed it

Why can't I wake up
my will feels strong
but I stumble about hurriedly
trying to shake my drugged body and mind
trying to find…

Ah, he's found it
at least I can dance to his music
now, he has fallen asleep
the record keeps turning
but I can no longer hear the music

If only I could awaken
I would know where to find it too.

Dream III

The dancers move forever before my eyes
dancing masks to adorn the shell
on and on new masks
brittle , grey unchangeable

They are the gifts of others
wear this one, now this
this is your shape, smell, colour

If only...

The music has stopped
the dancers begin to fade
the masks... a vanishing soft pulp

Who am I
you have stolen my identity
now only a dream...

If only we could remember the dream
we could find the memory of our self
not in the mathematics of words
or the measuring of ideas
but in the colour of sound
the smell of an image

Sometimes it is close
a phrase of music, smells of autumn
the colours in a painting
the sea...

But no, not that
those are all our dreams
our one large memory
memory of all our myth

But somewhere within these…
our dream
our self.

A Golden Voice

She stands there in a golden voice
making flowers bloom
stars rejoice
a drowned man tries to swim
singing her soul sings
while in a smoke filled room

The young chat wildly
in a sexual heat
the older sophisticates
talk business
compete
on a stock market gain

Then politely clap
as if they were there
never seeing her face
never feeling the rare
air

At the end of the night
she packs up
tiredly leaving the scene
passing "great honey", " you were terrific"
as she walks out
into a pre dawn rain

All she feels is the
fresh cleansing beauty
and knows that her rent will be paid
    and yes
    just a glimmer of joy
of the sounds she has made

She doesn't know
when she stands there
in a golden voice
that flowers bloom
stars rejoice
and a drowning man learns how to swim

Old Brown Grey Man

Old brown grey man
blackened nails
laceless boots
gnarled hands
crossed in pain?
or supplication?

Sits on a beach
does he dream of old memories?
perhaps no dreams at all
his body so quiet... watching
sensations, thoughts, pass through
leaving no trace
perhaps he has reached a state
        of grace
our downtown buddha

The Robes of Earth

She sits in the robes of earth
her hair the moon
her arms, lithe, gnarled limbs
        blossoming
legs the sea, tide flowing...
why, when you look, does the serpent
        snarl?

New Liberated Woman

Be careful, new liberated woman
for the moon will not allow
the desecration of her mysteries
her love-hate glow
contains the power of the night
be careful when you ignore her gift
for the womb is her sacred dancing ground
if your secret becomes barren
she will no longer dance.

The womb is the rhythm of the sea
the goldsmith smell of the dream
the memory of the dance…
the memory of an ancient melody
the he-she union of one.

Don't throw it away so easily
how can a temporal crown compare
when you have always worn the sacred crown?
don't give up the key to the final door.
If we lose the rhythm of our breath
we cannot beat the drum for celebration.

Poems for Plays

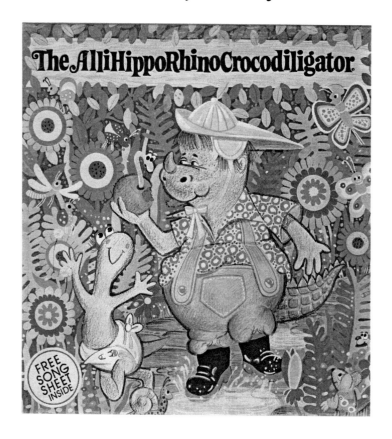

The AlliHippoRhinoCrocodiligator

FREE SONG SHEET INSIDE

Poems for Plays

This record was produced by Seashell Recordings, a division of Kaleidoscope Theatre Productions. It recorded 15 songs written by various members of the company, most of which were used in plays for children produced by the company.

Ralph Cole vocals, piano, guitar, concertina

Elizabeth Gorrie vocals and percussion

Paul Liittich vocals and percussion

Barb Poggemiller vocals and percussion

Ed.

Liz used her gift for writing poems as a way to verbalise the images that she wanted to use in her plays, particularly plays created for young children. Created, as opposed to written, is particularly appropriate for her work in this genre, as she worked with her casts as ensembles. Actors were encouraged to contribute to the creation of the play, and this would apply to the poems used as well as any other dialogue. These poems were often put to music, usually composed by a member of the cast. So it is appropriate to acknowledge these following examples of poems as collaborative pieces, which Liz orchestrated to explore the imagery that she wanted to use.

Mrs Ocean
Taken from The Allihipporhinocrocodiligator

Mrs Ocean takes in washing
every day the whole year thru'
and she uses so much bluing
that it stains the water blue

I've seen the suds a floating
when the waves were rough and high
but I never have discovered
where she hangs the clothes to dry

The waves come dancing full of fun
to play with me, then back they run
perhaps they hear their mother call
and so they do not stay at all

The waves are just like children
who are happy to run to you
their mother is the sea I know
for home to her they always go.

The Allihipporhinocrocodiligator

*Poem by Dan Costain and Barbara Poggemiller with
contributions from Paul Liittich and Barbara McLauchlin*

There's an Allihipporhinocrocodiligator here
sitting in the closet with a sock in his ear
do you think he's really happy?
does anybody care?
There's an Alihipporhinocrocadiligator here.

So the Allihipporhinocrocodiligator said
I'm going to the 'fridgerator for a slice of bread
a little pickle and some ketchup for my younger brother Fred
who's in the Alihipporhinocrocadiligator's bed

The Allihipporhinocrocodiligator went
for a walk in the puddles in some gumboots that he lent
to his uncle from Poughkeepsie in a loud Hawaiian shirt
on loan from the diligator's aunt named Gert

The Allihipporhinocrocodiligator swam
in a moat underwater all the way to the dam
with a snorkel and a mask and a guppie named Sam
I think that 'crocadiligator really is a ham

The Allihipporhinocrocodiligator danced
like a mad gypsy savage with ants in his pants
In his tutu and his point shoes and his fluffy pink pants
could that Allihipporhinocrocodiligator dance

So the Allihipporhinocrocodiligator sighed
and went back to the closet with some eggs that he fried
the kippers in his slippers smelled so bad that he cried
and the Allihipporhinocrocodiligator died.

Ed.
*This poem was put to music and recorded as the title song for
a vinyl of Kaleidoscope songs. It later became the title for a
Kaleidoscope production for young children. As noted it was not
written by Liz, but its authorship does reflect the way she worked
with her ensembles looking for creative input from all members of
the company. It would be remiss to have a selection of Liz's poems
used in her plays without this delightful piece of nonsense, the title
of which, incidentally, is usually easier for children to enunciate
and memorise than adults.*

*The word Allihipporhinocrocodiligator was credited to the
Times Colonist journalist Erith Smith. There are different
spellings of the word. This spelling was used on the record cover.*

Sea Shells
Taken from Where Umbrellas Bloom

My ears cannot distinguish
the words it sings to me
Sea shell, a wee shell
I hold so reverently
I only hear a whisper
like a ghost voice from the sea
Sea shell a wee shell
I hold so reverently

Sea shell, sea shell
sing me a song, oh please
a song of ships and sailor men
Islands lost in the Spanish Main
parrots and tropical trees
Sea shell. sea shell
sing me a song, oh please

A sea shell is a castle
where a million echoes roam
a wee castle, sea castle
tossed up by the foam
a wee creature's, sea creature's
long deserted home
a wee castle, sea castle
tossed up by the foam

Sea shell, sea shell
sing of the things you know
of fishes and corals in the waves
sea horses stabled in great green caves
lands where no one goes
Sea shell, sea shell
sing of the things you know.

Is it Possible?

Taken from Alice, *an adaptation of Lewis Carroll's two books,*
Alice in Wonderland *and* Alice Through the Looking Glass.

Is it possible the world outside
is larger than we see?
Have we blinkers on our eyes
our ears deaf to the trees?

Is it possible if time flies
it can dance on its head?
Or flowers do a minuet
while eating a slice of bread?
Is the rain just singing secrets
falling from the sky?
If we could only hear them
We could learn to fly.

Is it possible to open doors
to see a world never seen?
Rabbits wearing watches
that lead us to the Queen?
Chatting with the Doormouse
sleeping in her tea
travel on a flying train
flamingos, you and me?

Is it possible?

The Bi-Coloured-Python-Rock-Snake
Taken from Just So Stories

I'm a highly intelligent python
I don't get my tail in a knot
I'd rather discuss mathematics
than lie in the sun and just rot.

Slithering coiling 'round problems
my sliding and slippery mind
at your suggestion, can solve any question
'specially the difficult kind

A class act if ever I saw one
smooth as a tropical night
my velvety tongue will seduce you
my squeeze is much worse than my bite.

Ed.
This character is taken from The Elephant Child *in Rudyard Kipling's* Just So Stories, *some of which were used in Liz's adaptation for a theatre piece for children. Her poem was put to music by Michael Creber and used in the production.*
It was also used by her daughter's band Libeatos, with a more adult interpretation of the lyrics.

Political Thoughts

Political Thoughts

Paul Liittich's cartoon of Liz playing Sally Bowles in the musical *Cabaret*. Paul played the MC.

Multiculturalism

I love multi culture
it opens lovely wounds
poli incorrections
whistles fighting tunes
one good thing about it
whether black, or pink or rust
who in this human line up
moves to the back of the bus.

Yippi, okey dokey
I'm so glad I'm white
bigoted and blinkered
I keep moving to the right.

I love multi culture
its fun to ridicule
makes you look much smarter
makes them look the fool
try slurs like wop or slant eyes
and watch the feathers fly
without our multi culture
life is boring, life is dry.

Yippi, okey dokey
I'm so glad I'm white
bigoted and blinkered
I keep moving to the right.

Ed.
*Canada adopted a policy of multiculturalism when it was easy to
do so. The visible ethnic minorities were too small to cause any
problems.*

Easter Requiem
1 – Thou Shalt Not

The crucifix
The blood
Mutilation
Sacrifice

Wasn't love the message
that jump started this faith?
How did these icons
of terror begin?

Who's been calling the tune
over 2,000 years?

Grim reapers
in cassocks of black
building edifices, fortunes
to cover their fears
of demons about to attack

Attack what? and whom?
Whose demons? whose guilt?
what lie
lies underneath?

Half truths spoken
chanted for centuries
in angelic boys voices
and murmured endlessly
in the barren dry voices
of monks
and nuns
the sound of the wind
shifting dead bones
whispering
thou shalt not.

2 – Losing Innocence

On a quiet evening
a boy walks his dog
climbing the hill
he looks up at the stars
there's God shining,
the wonder fills his heart.
Yet
tomorrow is confession,
a different God
he's split apart

He plods home with heavy footsteps
the magic snuffed
the beauty blind.
He crawls up into his tiny bed
he must conjure up
the sins he's led.

continued...

The dog crawls up beside him
snuffling,
gently shoving
back into their nightly mould.
Half asleep
the boys arm goes round
he nuzzles then sighs asleep
on his neck.
For a moment the stars
and their wonder dance
the dreams
do the rest.

In the morning
dream wondered
a wet tongue
lapping his face
gently laughing awake
into his first
confession
of sin.

Let's Turn to Another Channel

Webs of thought
weaving through countless generations
more facts, more history
new processes, new moralities
the tapestry of the mind
saturated with infinite patterns and colours
until all spirals into a blur...
only the vaguest ideas form
let it go... no time...

Anyhow, we're informed
but it all goes on outside us now
we watch, fascinated
incapable
impotent
we watch our mind as a separate being
tortured, betrayed, lost
bouncing between unfamiliar hands
leaping and falling from dogma to fad
leaving us untouched

Couldn't I have it back?
oh no,... that would be painful
I don't like to feel pain

Let's turn to another channel.

The Dumpster Queen

Everyone knew her
tho' no one sees her
walking the streets with her cart
a true city woman
alone independent
collecting, then sleeping apart

Being a no one
she's refined so well
yet she rarely remembers her name
was it Katharine or Kate
or maybe Colleen?
a new one each day, is her game

Then one full moon night
at the edge of a dumpster
picking a survivor's dregs
a hand touched hers
she looked up in shock
to see eyes filled with hunger and dread

Terrified, she wanted to run
but something held her back
she turned, hearing his sobs
then gently cradled his body
cradled his lost
children and lives and jobs

You might notice them now
walking the streets
together, two carts lighter feet
but their lives will be short
both blood tainted souls
yet each day, each moment is sweet

No one knows
she was a writer of prose
and a poet lauded,
            esteemed
she fell through the
            cracks
            then
she found the man of
her dreams

So if you see them
hand out a toonie
more with a smile is best
to celebrate a moment
a dumpster moment
that sparked new hope, a new quest

Genocide

A nursery floor
strewn with tin soldiers
fallen forgotten
what the battle was about
when tea time was called

Rag dolls
limp arms and legs (splayed)
left
uncared for
in a heap
Nana, Amah
whatever her name
would pick them up
paint and sew
put them all back (again)
for tomorrow's game

Twenty year's later
the game's not the same
yet the players
don't notice
nothing has changed
tho' the bodies are real
soldiers red or blue
the dolls, raped
children abused
the only difference
is Nana's not there
to paint and sew
put them back
repaired

We're a kindly deadly race
shirt off your back
a knife through your face
a symphony plays
a soul soaring embrace
as ovens
exterminate a race

Humanity's still a dream
carried by those
bubble wrapped
in the safety
of wealth
in a place far removed

We're still on the survival trail
at any cost
the fittest prevail
the others are lost

Sure we pay our
donations to this
and to that
a moment of
recognition
the pain, the loss

Ed.
Written in response to the horrors of the civil war in Ruanda.

Flight 182

The decision's enormity
halts any thought!
for 20 years
the murdered families sought
an end
some justice
to the courtroom they came
wounds opened up
as each witness spoke
a spiral of lies
within this whirlpool
a truth
of some kind.

The sentence "not guilty"
witnesses instability
cited

The families gasp
unbelief and rage
the wounds bleeding
unstoppable
blood will react

How does he feel
the judge sitting alone
with a decision
weighing the truth
with the inconsistences
knowing they were
probably guilty
but the law
is larger than all of us
beheld to that and
beyond a reasonable doubt
he had to say
"not guilty"

Ed.
*On June 22, 1985 Air India Flight 182 flying from Montreal
to Delhi was blown up at an altitude of 31,000 feet killing 329
people, the first of such acts of political terror. Investigation and
prosecution took nearly 20 years with inconclusive results.*

It's Cowboy Time
Dedicated to George W

What we need boys
is rounding them up
get them in the corral
of democracy
any strays
seek them out
never mind the cost
a maverick bull
could endanger
our herd
      It's cowboy time

Okay, now boys
brand the steers
and the cows
with the triple "R"
Righteous
Rule
and Run
mighty smart
we've made our mark
      Cause it's cowboy time

Go home, now boys
you've done real well
enjoy a hit of bourbon
some pussy and pie
tomorrow
we take on our neighbour's herd
'cause they don't know what's best
in the freedom drive
      Yeah, it's cowboy time

We know what's best
don't we boys
we're democracy posses
out to save the world
from tyrants
sitting on liquid gold
let's free it up
be brave, be bold
      It's cowboy time

The Silence of Violence

A strange hush is happening
the birds are swarming
silently hovering
and all the horses have fled
from the carnival fair

A child awakes from a dream
tho' not dreaming
speaking in words unknown yet knowing
a street dweller hears the strange silence
so loud
he wanders to find some peace

A mother awakes in the still of the night
sweat drenched, begins to start baking
while around the world
millions toss and turn
allergies, indigestion or stress?
in the morning, thank god
the dis-ease is erased
by the radio/coffee hit
the caffeine and anchormen
assure us the world
is still fucked up but
we still exist

But the child and street dweller
know something else –
the strange silence surrounding the world
but neither are heard
in the smart 'with it' blur
of the stock market, fitness-right whirl

Yet...

The birds are swarming and silently hovering
the horses have flown the fair
they've peeled off the varnish
the make believe garnish
disappeared through the air in despair

Ed.
Written shortly before September 11th, 2001.

¾ Time

"faster and smarter and
sharper and "with it", and
"be there", "let's go there"
as the wind blows dead ashes
into the sun

We're alive and there's plenty of money
too bad for the guy in the street
'cause the kids, our financial investment
a nest egg, for us, so to speak.
So they do drugs and spend their allowance
on Levi's, CD's, and hashish
they've got their own cars, so they're free
free to scream down the road in dead heat.
So a pet here or there goes for nothing
and an old man crossing the street
wiped out in a miniscule second –
kid's highjinks, bailed out in a week.

But it's somebody's Rover or Grandpa
that's lost –irretrievably gone
and these kids are our sons and our daughters
Why this meaningless marathon?
Can't we teach them that life's about living?
Not gobbling up things on the run?
To be free is all about giving
the small seed that's fed by the sun.

I hear dry bones rattling around
snakes no longer shed their skins
as credit cards beat a dead rhythm
and lives held together with pins.

"faster and smarter and
sharper and "with it", and
"be there", "let's go there"
as the wind blows dead ashes
into the sun

Ed.
A comment on urban street racing and its wastage.

Past Teaches

Past Teaches

In 1990 Liz's choice of theme for the fundraising campaign brochure that built her theatre facility was taken from an anonymous quote: "Whatever else you leave undone, once, ride a wild horse into the sun!"

Scheherazade

Spin, spin
stitch and spin
weaving words
to offset the sin.

Choose colours so bright
they light up the night
ease the pain of the past
and the shadow it casts
each tale buys
another day in your life
sew each with wonder
sew each with delight.

Spin, spin
stitch and spin
weaving words
to offset sin.

Scheherazade
Queen of the night
weave your magic
to save your life
Scheherazade
fairy tale spinner
each thread designed
to absolve the sinner

Spin, apin
stitch and spin
weaving words
to offset sin.

Magdalena #1

The clowns have finished
their turn
to tepid
thanks from a crowd ....

Magdalena
          waits
at the bottom of the stairs
as the broken
lost angels
fall into her arms

They need that moment
of remembering glory
charms and laughter
covering a shiny
sequined nowhere

Magdalena
          holds their heads
          that break into
          pieces of past 'if onlys'

          holds their hands
          fluttering
          to grasp
          lost innocence

holds their dreams
that can't be held

She opens the window
gives them to the wind
watches them
play with the stars

Then a light
flutter and burst
into flames

A child's dream
is filled with laughter

The clown
unbelieving
gets better
and better
the child's laughter
goes on for ever

Magdalena smiles
forgiven again

Ed.
Liz was fascinated with Magdalena and Morgana, two women for
whom history has woven conflicting stories that show both sides of
their personalities.
Her notes indicate that she wanted to write much more about both
these women.

Morgana

Dare to go close
just a glimpse
causes madness
but I'll try again
once again

She's hidden herself
from a world
of such madness
there is nothing she can
regain
so she hides in the mists
exiled in a mythic
dream place
broken, lost
the battle between
holy church and the fathers
with their military might
who slaughtered the mothers
the daughters
so terrified by their sight

She lives in between
both worlds
what might and what is
chasing the 'isms'
men need to give
to their hauteur and slaughter
Oh yes she's there
past the veil that
will eat you
bone by bone
If you attempt to find her

vulnerable and alone
with conquest in your heart

She waits and grieves
her power, impotent
that power that terrifies
men
her cursed 'sight'
her shape changing magic
a boon to humanity
an earth healing balm
yet thru' centuries
denied, debased and
despised
her followers tortured and
burned

Still she watches and waits
as men orchestrate
their dances of death
again and again
her one great hope
was the Magdalena
a new world vision
of love

continued...

But the Magdalena's
traces from history
are lost
changed by the fathers
and all that we've got
is a whore
of no consequence

Yet a hint has been left
at the startling resurrection
the first witness
the first spoken words
the first to be chosen
and blessed with a path
to be taken.

Once again the fathers
muddied the waters
her place usurped
by the scribes and the brothers
cutting off an artery
of the life blood intended
to feed and empower
instead an amputated part
is what we're left with
like a crippled child
smart editors made their mark

Ed.
*Morgan Le Fay (Magician) was King Arthur's half-sister. History
has shown us two versions of who she was – villain and healer.*

The Funniest Man in the World Committed Suicide To-day

His face a thousand masks
charmed fingers wove miracles
from imaginations flask
creating worlds from bits of rope.
he flew on rainbows of laughter
wearing the jester's patched cloak
disarming clown, deadly wit
bon vivant, adventurer shit!

So what happened
to end his life as he did?
too much booze
fast closures –
too many silent guilts?
which must have
built and built
and built
and built

Was your pride too hard, too big?
and hung with a "keep out" sign?
those deft fingers changed their course
and dipped into the till at times
no longer creating
but shaking and taking
deeper and deeper in crime
so the game of shame
had to stop
but like that?

continued…

A star is gone
and the night sky is different
a light's out
forever
it's darker than before
so I want to roar
and soar
and war

Damn him!

The funniest man in the world
committed suicide to-day
hung by a rope
his deft fingers fashioned
not whimsical shapes
to delight the senses
but knotted with a deadly passion.

Ed.
The trio who established Kaleidoscope Theatre Company were a journalist corralled into manager, a designer turned actor and a director who started writing. The creative leadership between Paul and Liz lasted for over a decade. But with all creative partnerships there came a time to separate. Without any call for help Paul's death was difficult to digest.

Left to right: Peter Hall, Paul Liittich, Sam Mancuso.
Clowns, written and directed by Liz Gorrie, 1981.

In Memory of Anne Bonny – Pirate
An Afterthought

1.
At the edge of my mind is a horror
can we change the steps
to the dance of death?
I need wilder angels
those in a picture frame
with no picture
that bursts into flames at a glance
running on sand, leaving no tracks
tragic magic
fireworks ejaculating against the sky
of my mind

2.
I sit in this cell
putrid, dank
dark shadows dance
cross my eyes
on my soul
for a moment my mind
soars on the billows
of sea free
then dragged down
down
by the tow
too much life
too much death

The price of freedom
is dear
yet, I would do it again

3.
Absolution, forgiveness?
don't make me laugh!
measuring deeds
is a milksop's task
I broke the rules of the game
the air becomes sharper
the mind is aflame
now walk the abyss
cruelty, ecstasy
once burned into the soul
there's no going back

The price of freedom
is dear
and yet....
and yet...

4.
Two candle flames
defy me
and try me,
the wick splutters
then revives
I see my father
grey haired
mind wandering
through hallways of madness
searching and calling
"my lad shall have freedom
unfettered, unshackled
where are you, my son
my Anne?"

5.
To live the life he was
born to
on bended knee
he prays for his lad
as he sets the plantation
on fire
his last words
carried on the breeze
to me
release my son
my Anne

Yes I am
Anne Bonny
Queen of Pirates
Devil of the High Seas

The price of freedom
is dear
but I'll do it again

6.
Mary, my gentle
allowing arms lullaby fears
making me weak
to a world no longer mine
I'll hear you cry
from the grave
for all time

These twin flames
could shatter the mirror
the blasted vision
Oh
the price of freedom
is dear
and I would do it again

7.
I'm a ship
can't be landlocked
my mind's filled with winds
my heart straddles the topsail
feeding on vast horizons
ropes, stanchions hold strong
not tying me down
not making a jest
of a human heart
flying on the crest of impossible

8.
I've killed those I loved
and I loved some I've slain
but I've sailed to my soul
seen it's dark light
without shame

Yes
the price of freedom
is dear
but I would do it again

continued...

9.
No corsets to shackle
no hair teased and tidy
no shoes pinched and perfect
to scotch an escape
keep your brittle moralities
your shriveled souls
the doors of your petty prisons
won't hold

10.
While I sit here in this cell
putrid and dank
twin flames let me go
cut the ropes
unfurl the sail
leap and the net will appear

The price of freedom
is dear
and I will do it again.

Ed.
Liz finished her last play, Anne Bonny, *a few months before she died, based on what is known of the extraordinary history of this female pirate. This poem was her afterthought.*

Betrayal

Is there some sickness in your soul
as she plays you
eating you alive

Is there some sickness in your soul
that pulls you
to her darkness
forgetting so quickly
your beauty recognized
by fellow sufferers

Is there a sickness in your soul
that leaves only a mirage
of your return
to humour
shared moments
of pain
of joy
of terror
release

Is there a sickness in your soul
that betrayal of those
who love you
stood by you
are like dandelion fluff
blown
scattered in the wind
that cannot smell the putrid
rotting of her lies

continued...

Is there a sickness in your soul
that silences the tears
of your son
your mother
father
sister
friends
who have fought for you and your soul

Yes there is a sickness
and her name you know

Is she only the first skin
on the onion
peel another layer
do you dare
to find another
darkness there

But maybe
a gentle light
still glows
surrounding
that was
that is
You

Looking Back

Looking Back

Shakespeare's *Pericles, Prince of Tyre*, directed by Liz Gorrie in Kaleidoscope's new theatre, October, 1993.

The Last Laugh

If it's the last laugh
who has it?
as the dice are tossed
fingers crossed
playing your life
on the odds

Do you want a
good bookie
do you
want to
win or
lose?

It's your last laugh
you can choose

But dancing on shifting sands
of your mind
can whisper
your soul away
just as her breath
leaves wisps of
brimstone
evil has passed your way

Puppet
or puppeteer
who plays the strings?
(It could be
your choice)

For Mother
(and the rest of us)

How grand she looks
in contemplation
the profile patrician
her world in its place

You don't see the body
shriveled
locked into a monstrous
padded huge baby car seat
where she sits for hours
living her past
now her present

Confronting her
in our 'real' presence
confuses
she needs to act
"Are we driving home for Christmas?
We need to make plans"
Then her social mother rises
"Pour us a drink
I'm not sure what's in the kitchen
I haven't shopped for days
I'll find something
Ssurely you will stay?"
Dementia hasn't eroded deep habits.

How do you tell her?
she'll be wheeled down to eat
in her monstrous car seat
while you make a retreat

Fleeing the pain
the obscenity of a life
decomposing
get away, drink a lot
'cause your life's still existing
hide the reality deep
not of death
but the ending of life
so degraded

Playing a game of crib
the game memory's strong
but lucid's a curse now
she puts down her cards
saying
"I'm not feeling well"
at that moment I realized
she knew her mind's gone
she glimpsed again
into her personal hell

Thankfully, that dark knowledge
is lost in a shifting mist
of time out of time
or a time we can't see

continued…

Yet her beauty is startling
tho' her eyes are dim
there's a gentleness
a certain peace
that's new
is it dementia or
something we can't know?
Another mystery of life
we haven't plumbed? *
can't know, can't follow

And now
the last journey
the final journey
and tho' we can't see
I'm sure flights of angels
guide her home
and bow their heads
at such dignity

Author's note
plumbed... the word plumbed is there for my grandfather, Pappy.
Being a mason, that was part of his trade and one of his favorite
words.

Lynn Wallace 1908–2008

Feb 14, '59

A costume dance – I was Carmen
I don't remember your mask –
but we danced, not always together
it was all dancing and dancing the dance.
Next morning – how did I get there?
An 8.30 Saturday class
but you drove me home, mascara traces
left on my face as I glanced –
as you walked from the car
on an errand
the white chimera of truth
pierced my soul
this man is my path, my lover
forever to love and to hold.

Forty years later
the vision proved truer than others
less strong
through betrayals, children
and broken dreams
our love is a triumphant song
the give and the take
the holder and the holded
the dance with few mis-steps goes on

So perhaps we should thank that chimera
who took over my soul and holds on
but do you remember what day it was?
when my heart was captured
and bound?
Feb 14 '59
yes, Valentine's Day, love was found

Saying Goodbye to a Friend

Letting go,
old friend
put you out to pasture
the hardest
choice of my life

You were always there
in stress
in laughter
deep conversations
and terror of failure

You were there for
a moment of rest
apart from
the needs
to pool my resources

You were there for
a moment alone
too much family
too much, too much
just standing alone
watching the night sky

But
I've relied on you
too often
too many years
you've been my prop
beautiful but deadly
you're killing me
must stop

Our dance, a perfect tango
we knew each other's needs
our bodies found each other
to create, realize dreams

So this is a "dear John" letter

I have to say goodbye
we've had exciting
coaster rides
we've played the odds
we've won and lost

But
I can no longer
be your bride
you're killing me.

The last cigarette.

Gypsy Go Home

The gypsies
camp out
at the edge of my soul
waiting ....
Oh how they
know how to wait

Disappearing for years
then suddenly return
with the lure
of a melancholy violin
melting the scar
of a sadness I don't want
a passion
that cannot begin again

Free
flying
staccato feet
pounding the earth
wild abandon
round and round
the sound of my blood
pulsing singing
I'm alive

I see the knife raised
blood flowing
as the violin
strives to heights
of never before
and I'm riding on a steed
racing through the night
pounding, throbbing
into the dawn

The violins have died
only a sad wind
rustles my tattered gown
as I sit
a noble head
dying in my lap
my tears mixing
in his last blood

Gypsies stay away
don't come close
I'll live without passion
even without hope

Go home
I choose peace

Ed.
An unanswered question posed by the author in her notes on this
poem. '…have to make clear why I am riding on a horse so the
path of such a death is clear.' The answer, perhaps, is in another
poem, The Great Steed.

Choose

The carousel's spinning
it's always been there
at the back or the front of the mind
but try to ignore it
now you don't want it
the dials refuse to obey.
turn off, turn down but
the calliope sounds
keep coming in and out.

It draws you
demands
to walk to the edge
of the merry-go-round
go round
walk to the edge
to the horse painted black
eyes fierce, legs extended
the wild steed
that could drive you insane

Can you stop
not pick up the reins?

Choose!
you can do it
turn away, don't get on
tho' other voices are
urging you on to
voices deeply beloved
true, and rarely
wrong
but they've never ridden
this wild black steed
they don't know
that this time round
it's likely that death
is as certain
as dawn

Colin
March 3, 2005

I see your head
on the pillow
next to mine
and I want to stop time
tho' grey in your hair
and muscles
adonis lapsed
a life time of beauty
reaches out in each breath
can it be that our time
is running out?

We've danced our lives together
sometimes foolish
sometimes brave
but dancing's how we did it
missteps faltering
but again, yet again
we picked up the rhythm
fell in step
twirled and whorled
danced to the music
with one heart

If the pillow
next to me is bare
the dance ended
musicians gone
I'll laugh and cry
and join you there
waiting somewhere
on another stair

Just a fantasy
earth bound souls grasp
need to hold?
Or does love
go to another place?
Unknown
we'll never know.

Looking on Life

To feel in the centre
to be a part
where the pulse beats
beating your rhythm
finger tips tapping the heart
ideas flow free
as a west coast rain
heavy with passion
or misted lightly
with a melancholy
that has no name

Instead, I watch and walk
greedily glimpsing through windows
lit with amber glows – possibilities
of lives filled with directions
with drives
with desires
only a life voyeur now
vicarious
tenuous
and outside

It's not cold
it's not uncomfortable
it's easy
it's safe
it's nice

Yet the images of wine and laughter
arguments and despair
the razor's edge on a tightrope
falling into applause at the end
but it's not the reveling the kudos
nor the joy of a summit just won

It's the silence
a blank piece of paper
as if I'd never been there

I'll not go back to the centre
and my fingers won't tap at the heart
wine and laughter will lose its edge

But maybe that's a start…

Staring Death Down

How do you stare
death in the face?

With an exercised
food right body?
Is it all a dream
a nightmare
soon to wake
remembering
a terror
that's true

How do you stare
death in the face?
with children
to care for
and a love
far from finished?

How DO you stare
death in the face?

Can you stare it down?
Can you say
"Flee, go away
Its too soon"
or
"Not me
You've made a mistake"
Or
"Just fuck off!"

How do you stare
death in the face?

Open your mouth
wide
suck death in
chew slowly
and
spew it out
with fingers crossed
bravado high
say
"find another loser
more likely
to fall
for
your dark deadly arms."

Walk the Streets of Forever
A love song for old lovers

Time
running out
a love so deep
that death can separate?
Yes
the way of the world
spirals us into
the other, maybe into
stardust.
so our hands
will never clasp again
my head on your
chest
will never know
again feel
the pulse of your heartbeat
the smell of your skin.

If only we could fly
together into netherland
and walk the streets
of forever

As the Crows So I

At ease
as the temperature
drops
pleasant
almost euphoric
watching the crows
nightly patter
flying east

I always worry
about the stragglers
a mother, a father
going back to find
a lost child?

Tonight the moon
is almost full
I can smell the sea
close by
gaze at a city
so beautiful
it sometimes takes
my breath away

and yet I am
saying goodbye
goodbye
to my country of birth
goodbye
to a beauty
so profound

continued…

poets struggle
and try to grasp
the air
sea colours
mountain horizons
eagles soaring
inlets, fjords
forever
into new worlds

I have chosen to
go back
back
to an old world
to find what?
something
that's missing
something old

I do need to find
Avalon
ancestors
old magic
I need the
pulse of
past generations
eons of souls

This the last step
the final journey?

Liz Gorrie's Professional Theatre Career

* Written or adapted by Liz Gorrie
# Directed by Liz Gorrie
x Performed

Glenhurst Theatre Guild, Brantford, Ontario
1968–69 # Scrooge – The Stingiest Man in Town
Tom Jones by Joan Macalpine

Total Theatre Brandford, Ontario
1969–70 # America Hurrah – Jean-Claude van Itallie
The Purification – Tennessee Williams
x Cabaret – John Kander and Joe Masteroff
1970–71 # The Royal Pardon – John Arden &
Marguerite D'Arcy
The Serpent – Jean-Claude van Itallie

Bastion Studio Theatre, Victoria, British Columbia
1971–72 # Peer Gynt – Ibsen
Trojan Women – Euripides
The Night Thoreau Spent in Jail – Lawrence
& Lee
#x Jacque Brel (musical revue)

Kaleidoscope Theatre, Victoria, British Columbia
1974–75 *# The Musicians of Bremen
1975–76 *# Oriental Legend
*# The Allihipporhinocrocodilagator
*# The Legend of the Minotaur
*# Snow Goose (adapted from Paul Gallico's
novella)
*# The Book Show (commissioned by Victoria
Public Library)
x Cabaret – John Kander and Joe Masteroff

1976–77 *# Slechie Song
*# Rutabaga Country
*# Kaleidophonics 1 (commissioned by the
Victoria Symphony)
*# The Garden Show
*# The Way we Were (commissioned by
the Royal BC Museum)
x Jacques Brel (musical revue)
1977–78 # Peer Gynt – Ibsen
*# Salt the Seas and Pepper the Mints
*# A Victorian Christmas (commissioned by
the Royal BC Museum)
*# Mon Pays, My Country
* Steam (commissioned by Royal BC Museum)
1978–79 *# Sumidagawa
Jeremiah's Place – George Ryga
*# Kaleidophonics 2 (commissioned by the
Victoria Symphony)
*x Songs of the Cabaret (musical revue)
(tent summer theatre)
1979–80 *x Songs of the Cabaret (moved to Red Lion
Inn)
*# About Free Lands (commissioned by
Museum of Man & Nature, Winnipeg)
*# Nightmares and other Horses (Dreams)
*# Merlin's Quest
*# Kaleidophonics 3 (commissioned by the
Victoria Symphony)
1980–81 *# Clowns
*# About Free Lands
*# The Library Show (commissioned by
Victoria Public Library)
1981–82 # Snow Goose (National Children's Theatre,
Tel Aviv, Israel)
*# Unicorns
*# Kaleidophonics 4

1982–83   *# Where Umbrellas Bloom
         *# Kaleidophonics 5
1983–84   *# Alice (adaptation of Lewis Caroll stories)
         *# Noel
         # Unicorns (National Children's Theatre,
         Tel Aviv, Israel)
1984–85   * The Tempest – Shakespeare
         *# Alice (remount for tour)
1985–86   *# Stepping Out
         *# Games of the World (commissioned
         Vancouver's International Children's Festival)
         * Hajamari No Hajamari (# Yukio Sekiya)
         North American tour
1986–87   # Hajamari No Hajamari (tour in Japan)
         #* Kaleidophonics 6
1987–88   * Three Musketeers (adaptation of Alexandre
         Dumas novel)
         *# Kaleidophonics 7
1988–89   *# Kaleidophonics 8 (remount for tour)
1989–90   *# Callanish
         * Romeo and Juliet – Shakespeare
1990–91   *# Hans Christian Anderson Stories
         Opening season at the new Kaleidoscope
         Theatre
1991–92   *# Midsummer Nights' Dream
         *# Victorian Christmas
         * Reader's Theatre
1992–93   *# Alice (adaptation of Lewis Carroll stories)
         # The Brontes – Roger Maybank
1993–94   # Pericles – Shakespeare
         * Lets Do Munsch (adaptation)
         *# Wizard of Earthsea (adaptation of Ursula
         Le Guin's novel)
1994–95   * Let's do Munsch Again
         *# Tehanu (adaptation of Ursula Le Guin's novel)

1995–96 # Romeo and Juliet – Shakespeare
         *# Stilletto
1996–97 # Temple of Stars – Marilyn Bowering
         # Gulliver's Travels – adapted by Christopher
         Weddell
         *# White Jade Tiger (adapted from Julie
         Lawson's novel)
1997–98 *# Just So Stories (adapted from Rudyard
         Kipling)
         *# Diner at the End of the Galaxy
1998–99 *# Callanish
         *# The Grinch who stole Christmas (adapted
         from Dr Suess)
         *# Allihipporhinocrocodillagator
2000   # City (High School musical)

Scripts Available
Created, written or adapted by Liz Gorrie

For further information, please contact Colin Gorrie at:
Flat 13, Shorland House, Beaufort Road, Bristol, BS8 2JT UK
colincgorrie@gmail.com 44 (0)1179 049 137

Alice
Alihippocrocadiligator
Anne Bonny – female pirate
Calanish
Just So Stories
Kaleidophonics – a symphony show
Merlin
Mon Pays, My Country
Oriental Legend
Peer Gynt – adaptation of Ibsen's play
Rutabaga Country
Selchie Song
*Snow Goose
Sumidagawa – a Japanese legend
Tales from Hans Christian Anderson
The Ant and the Grasshopper
Unicorns
Where Umbrellas Bloom
*White Jade Tiger
*Wizard of Earthsea

* To use these scripts would require permission from the authors of the novels adapted.

Liz's notes for her adaptation of Shakespeare's *The Tempest* and *Romeo and Juliet* are also available.

It should also be noted that some of the scripts, in particular those for young children, were the results of ensemble work and incorporate contributions from those actors.

CPSIA information can be obtained at www.ICGtesting.com
Printed in the USA
BVOW020806020412

286613BV00001B/4/P